O'REILLY®

Strata
MAKING DATA WORK

O'Reilly Strata is the essential source for training and information in data science and big data—with industry news, reports, in-person and online events, and much more.

- **Weekly Newsletter**
- **Industry News & Commentary**
- **Free Reports**
- **Webcasts**
- **Conferences**
- **Books & Videos**

Dive deep into the latest in data science and big data.
strataconf.com

©2014 O'Reilly Media, Inc. The O'Reilly logo is a registered trademark of O'Reilly Media, Inc. 131041

Analyzing the Analyzers
An Introspective Survey of Data Scientists and Their Work

Harlan D. Harris, Sean Patrick Murphy, and Marck Vaisman

O'REILLY®

Beijing · Cambridge · Farnham · Köln · Sebastopol · Tokyo

Analyzing the Analyzers

by Harlan D. Harris, Sean Patrick Murphy, and Marck Vaisman

Copyright © 2013 Harlan D. Harris, Sean Patrick Murphy, and Marck Vaisman. All rights reserved.

Printed in the United States of America.

Published by O'Reilly Media, Inc., 1005 Gravenstein Highway North, Sebastopol, CA 95472.

O'Reilly books may be purchased for educational, business, or sales promotional use. Online editions are also available for most titles (*http://my.safaribooksonline.com*). For more information, contact our corporate/institutional sales department: 800-998-9938 or *corporate@oreilly.com*.

Editor: Mike Loukides

June 2013:   First Edition

Revision History for the First Edition:

2013-06-06:   First release

See *http://oreilly.com/catalog/errata.csp?isbn=9781449371760* for release details.

Nutshell Handbook, the Nutshell Handbook logo, and the O'Reilly logo are registered trademarks of O'Reilly Media, Inc. *Analyzing the Analyzers* and related trade dress are trademarks of O'Reilly Media, Inc.

Many of the designations used by manufacturers and sellers to distinguish their products are claimed as trademarks. Where those designations appear in this book, and O'Reilly Media, Inc., was aware of a trademark claim, the designations have been printed in caps or initial caps.

While every precaution has been taken in the preparation of this book, the publisher and authors assume no responsibility for errors or omissions, or for damages resulting from the use of the information contained herein.

ISBN: 978-1-449-37176-0

[LSI]

Table of Contents

1. Introduction... 1
2. Case Studies in Miscommunication........................ 5
   Rock Stars and Gods   5
   Apples and Oranges   6
3. A Survey of, and About, Professionals................... 9
   Clustering Data Scientists   10
     Self-Identification   10
     Skills   11
     Combining Skills and Self-ID   12
   The Variety of Data Scientists   14
     Data Businesspeople   14
     Data Creatives   15
     Data Developer   15
     Data Researchers   16
   Big Data   16
   Related Surveys   17
4. T-Shaped Data Scientists................................ 19
   Evidence for T-Shaped Data Scientists   20
5. Data Scientists and Organizations....................... 23
   Where Data People Come From: Science vs. Tools Education 23
   From Theory to Practice: Internships and Mentoring   24
   Teams and Org Charts   25

| Career Paths | 26 |

6. Final Thoughts... **27**

A. Survey Details... **29**

CHAPTER 1
Introduction

Binita, Chao, Dmitri, and Rebecca are data scientists. What does that statement tell you about them? Probably not as much as you'd like. You know they probably know something about statistics, programming, and data visualization. You'd hope that they had some experience finding insights from data, maybe even "big data." But if you're trying to find the best person for a job, you need to be more specific than just "doctor," or "athlete," or "data scientist." And that's a problem. Finding the right people for a task is all about efficient communication and, without the appropriate shared vocabulary, data science talent and data science problems are too often kept apart.

The three of us, organizers of data science events in Washington, DC (*http://datacommunitydc.org/*), decided that we wanted to do something about this problem after too many personal experiences of failures caused by miscommunication. So in mid-2012 we surveyed data scientists, asking about their experiences and how they viewed their own skills and careers. The results may help us, as a professional community, settle on finer-grained descriptions and more effective means of communicating about what we do for a living.

We start by describing four fictitious data scientists, each typical of one of four categories that emerged from the survey. Their variety is striking.

Binita works for Acme Industries — a Fortune 100 manufacturing company — as Director of Analytics. She manages a small team of technical analysts and spends rather more time in meetings than she wishes. She really likes getting her hands dirty, diving into data sets when she has time, and helping her team design compelling visualizations and predictive models that will go into production. But the payoff is the presentation to senior management, translating statistical jargon to business lingo, *p*-values into profits. Binita has a bachelors in Industrial Engineering and an MBA, and she spent several years in consulting before moving to her role at Acme. She reads all about the new "big data" and "data science" buzzwords in the business press, and sees value in her skills, but isn't sure which labels apply to her. Maybe she'll start an analytics consulting firm of her own soon?

Chao has a finger in every pie. By day he builds interactive web graphics for a major newspaper, but by night he goes to technical Meetups and works on an open-source Python package for mapping spatial data. A few times a year he goes to hackathons, teaming up with others to prototype new businesses or dive into public data sets. Chao has an undergraduate degree in economics, minoring in computer science. He started a Master's in statistics before dropping out and trying unsuccessfully to start a statistical consulting firm. He's been following the blogs and tweets about data science since 2009, and his business cards (the ones he made on Moo with colorful data visualizations, not the boring ones he gets from work) say "Chao, Data Scientist Extraordinaire!"

Dmitri writes really fast, elegant, maintainable Machine Learning code. He works for a medium-sized consulting firm that provides predictive models for companies without the resources to build systems themselves. The skills section of his resume has five dense lines of technologies like Hadoop, SVM, and Scala. Dmitri keeps up with the Machine Learning literature, which he started reading when he was writing his Master's thesis in computer science. He's contributed a few patches to an open source big data package that he uses in his work. Dmitri is pretty happy with his job, but imagines he'll find a different development job in a few years. Maybe something using Dremel or other massive columnar databases — that stuff looks pretty cool.

Rebecca works for an internet retailer and has the title Data Scientist. Ten years ago if you had asked her what she'd be doing now, she'd have said, "I guess I'll be a professor by then." After spending 10 years studying molecular biology, building statistical models, programming simulations, managing complex data sets, publishing papers, and presenting at conferences, she decided she was bored. Rebecca left her post-doc and started farming out her resume, tweaking the language based on articles she'd read about the need for data science in industry.

Now she helps the company figure out which marketing practices are actually useful, builds predictive models of future sales, and looks for relevant patterns in Twitter data. Fun stuff! She still gets to read academic papers, learn new tools, and play with a vast array of data. But now her insights get noticed, and her work turns into real changes in the business.

Why do people use the term "data scientist" to describe all of these professionals? Does it clarify expectations, distinguish people with different strengths, and let practitioners and organizations communicate effectively and make good decisions? Does it define an attainable career path and suggest professional growth options? Or does it instead lead to confusion, misunderstandings, and missed opportunities?

We think that terms like "data scientist," "analytics," and "big data" are the result of what one might call a "buzzword meat grinder." The people doing this work used to come from more traditional and established fields: statistics, machine learning, databases, operations research, business intelligence, social or physical sciences, and more. All of those professions have clear expectations about what a practitioner is able to do (and not do), substantial communities, and well-defined educational and career paths, including specializations based on the intersection of available skill sets and market needs. This is not yet true of the new buzzwords. Instead, ambiguity reigns, leading to impaired communication (Grice, 1975 (*http://en.wikipedia.org/wiki/Cooperative_principle*)) and failures to efficiently match talent to projects.

In the rest of this article, we'll see how miscommunication about data science skills and roles led to wasted time and effort for Dmitri and Binita. We'll use the survey results to identify a new, more precise vocabulary for talking about their work, based on how data scientists describe themselves and their skills. We'll discuss how data scientists are both broad and deep and what this means for career growth and effectiveness. And finally, we'll turn from the practitioner's to the organization's point of view and consider how to apply the survey results when trying to identify, train, integrate, team up, and promote data scientists.

CHAPTER 2
Case Studies in Miscommunication

There are two related issues that we have seen when it comes to misunderstandings about the roles of data scientists. In one case, excessive hype leads people to expect miracles, and miracle-workers. In the other case, a lack of awareness about the variety of data scientists leads organizations to waste effort when trying to find talent. These case studies are based on collective experiences from many of our friends, colleagues, and Meetup members.

Rock Stars and Gods

Dmitri, our machine learning developer, gets head-hunted by a successful e-commerce company that has now realized the need for a data scientist. The recruiter supplies the following job description:

> We're looking for a Data Scientist Superstar to revolutionize the online experience. Are you excited about leveraging state-of-the-art methods to turn big data into business value? Can you manage people and projects and see an idea through from conception to delivery?

The rest of the job description shows a laundry list of desired skills, including terms like "Big Data," a dozen algorithm names, and other jargon. Dmitri thinks that this looks pretty reasonable and is comfortable that he meets the vast majority of the requirements. He has several phone interviews and is invited onsite.

During the first few minutes of Dimitri's meeting with the CEO, it becomes clear that they are looking for much more than what was previously discussed. Dmitri asks politely for more details about what the CEO is really seeking, and the CEO calmly responds "I want GOD! I want a rockstar programmer who has developed highly sophisticated machine learning algorithms, has built a distributed back-end big data platform, and has started a company!"

Dmitri respectfully responds back: "I wish you the best of luck finding that person." These expectations are highly unreasonable — at least for a single person — so Dmitri decides to pass on the opportunity. The expectation of miracles does not place the company, nor Dmitri, in a good position.

In his next interview with a small but exciting startup, Dmitri's interview with the CEO is much less eventful and more productive. However, after wrapping up his interview with the CTO, he is informed that the next step in the process is a fun project that should only consume a few hours: find a publicly available data set at least several hundred gigabytes in size, pose and answer an interesting question about the data, and detail all steps, assumptions, and conclusions, including code. If this request is coming from the technically savvy CTO, Dmitri wonders what other unrealistic expectations this position may entail.

Apples and Oranges

Binita's job search illustrates a different problem. As a data-savvy manager with an updated resume, she is recruited constantly for data scientist roles. However, the last three interviews ended the same way; organizations label the position as "Data Science" but want a new member to join an existing software engineering team to write production-level code.

In one case, Binita begins a conversation with a well-known technology company. She is initially concerned that the position is too technical but is assured by the manager that they want a senior person who can develop business strategies and performance metrics, as well as talk algorithms. Binita can build prototypes, but she does not code production-level software. Concerned, she flies out to the West coast anyway.

Upon arrival, her trepidation only increases as she is not scheduled to meet a single business person. A technical interviewer walks in, introduces himself, and then dives into the first question: "Tell me, what are B-trees, how do they work, and how does the SQL query optimizer use them?" While Binita has heard of this data structure, her job has never required this knowledge, and the rest of the allotted interview time is spent awkwardly. Needless to say, Binita does not get the job.

Unlike Dmitri's experiences, the problem here is not that the company was looking for a major deity but that it failed to communicate clearly the role's required skills, costing both the potential candidate and the company significant time and expenses.

CHAPTER 3
A Survey of, and About, Professionals

How can we, as a professional community, fix this problem? Perhaps by using the tools we know best — data collection, data analysis, and data communication. In mid-2012, the three of us set out to do some old-school data science and constructed a survey of practitioners. But not just any survey. We wanted to ask questions that would help us understand and define sub-groups — not based on years of experience, or academic degrees, or titles — but based instead on how data scientists think about themselves and their work. We didn't ask about verticals, or pay scales, or org charts. We avoided tool and technique questions about database platforms or favorite statistical or machine learning techniques. Others have asked those questions, and the answers are interesting, but not relevant to our problem.

We created a five-page web survey, taking less than 10 minutes to complete and focusing on five areas: skills, experiences, education, self-identification, and web presence. (Regarding web presence, we asked for those willing to share their LinkedIn, Meetup, and GitHub profiles, so that we could perform additional text analysis. However, due to relatively low response rates and some technical issues, the results were not usable, and will not be reported.) After testing the survey on a small group of friends and colleagues, we shared it broadly, evangelized it to professional Meetups, and posted links on every relevant social network we could think of. By the end of the project, we received over 250 completed surveys from around the globe. (See Appendix: "Design and Invitation" on page 29 for more details.) Our first task was to look for underlying clusters in our respondents — clusters that may be the basis for new ways to communicate about data scientists, their careers, and their roles.

Clustering Data Scientists

Two sets of survey questions lent themselves to a clustering analysis. We asked respondents to rank a diverse set of data science-related skills, and we also asked the extent to which they self-identified with a variety of professional categories.

Self-Identification

How do you think about yourself and your career? How might you talk about yourself to friends, colleagues, or potential employers? To gain insight, we asked people to state the extent to which they agreed with 11 "I think of myself as a/an X" statements (Figure 3-1) using a standard five-level Completely Agree to Completely Disagree scale.

Data Developer	Developer	Engineer	
Data Researcher	Researcher	Scientist	Statistician
Data Creative	Jack of All Trades	Artist	Hacker
Data Businessperson	Leader	Businessperson	Entrepeneur

Figure 3-1. Respondents tended to agree or disagree consistently to questions such as "I think of myself as a/an X" in each Self-ID Group. Our suggested Self-ID Group names are shown, along with the self-ID categories most strongly associated with each Group.

As discussed in more detail in Appendix: "Non-negative Matrix Factorization", we identified four clusters (latent factors) in our responses. Each cluster is a set of self-ID categories that people tended to respond to consistently. For example, it was unlikely that an individual data scientist would both agree strongly that they are a Statistician but disagree strongly that they are a Scientist. We named the four clusters to be evocative of the range of self-ID categories most associated with that cluster. These named clusters we define as Self-ID Groups. Note that each self-ID category was most strongly associated with a single Self-ID Group, with the exception of Jack of All Trades, which is only narrowly most associated with the Data Creative group. We will describe each of these Self-ID Groups in more detail below, but first we want to introduce Skills Groups.

Skills

What skills do you bring to your work? What are your primary areas of expertise? It can be tricky to get good answers to these questions. On a scale of 1 to 10, how good are you at Math? Rather than try to get comprehensible answers to this nearly incomprehensible question, we elected to ask respondents to rank their skills. This is a lot easier. As applied to your work, are you more skilled at Visualization or at Bayesian/Monte Carlo Statistics?

We developed a set of 22 generic skills that we thought spanned the range of useful things that data scientists might do in their work (Figure 3-2). A few concrete examples were provided with each skill to clarify and to aid ordering (see Appendix: "Skills List"). Respondents dragged-and-dropped those skills into an ordered list, with their introspectively determined top skill on top.

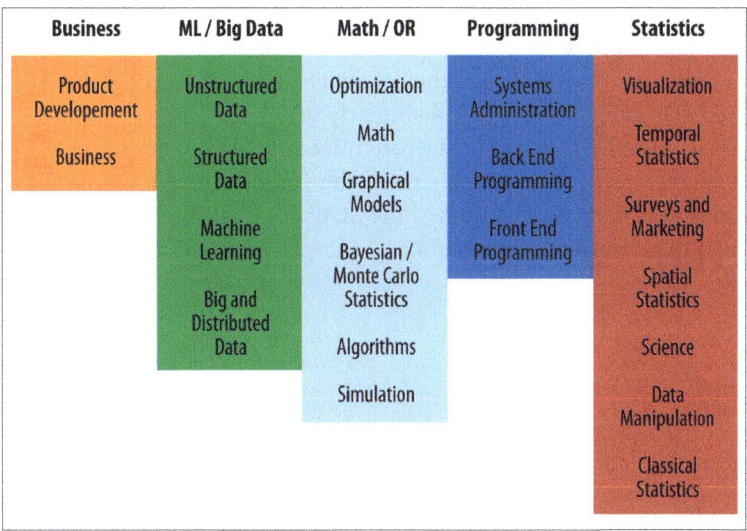

Figure 3-2. Respondents tended to rank similarly skills in each Skills Group. Our suggested Skills Goup names are shown, along with the skills most strongly associated with each Group. ML = "Machine Learning" and OR = "Operations Research."

As with the Self-ID Groups, we clustered the Skills, providing names for each cluster to summarize those skills concisely. For example, respondents tended to rank Spatial Statistics and Surveys and Marketing together, either ranking both relatively high or both relatively low. As before, most Skills categories were most strongly associated with a single Skills Group, with two exceptions. Structured Data, which ended up in the ML/Big Data Skills group, was also strongly associated with the Programming skills group. And Machine Learning, which also ended up with the ML/Big Data group, was also commonly ranked highly by respondents who ranked Math/OR or Statistics skills highly.

It's worth noting that because we used rankings instead of an absolute scale, we are not suggesting that two data scientists who rank ML/Big Data skills highly are equivalently skilled or effective. One may be a recent university graduate, having only completed coursework in Machine Learning, while another may have decades of experience applying these techniques to a wide range of problems.

Combining Skills and Self-ID

Figure 3-3 shows how our respondents fell into our four Self-ID Groups and five Skills Groups. Each respondent's responses can be "compressed" by replacing their eleven Self-ID ratings with their four Self-ID Group loadings, and similarly for Skills. The respondent can then be labeled by their most strongly loaded Self-ID and Skills groups. For example, someone who rated the Data Businessperson Self-ID questions highest, and ranked the Statistics Skills highest, would fall into the lower-left rectangle.

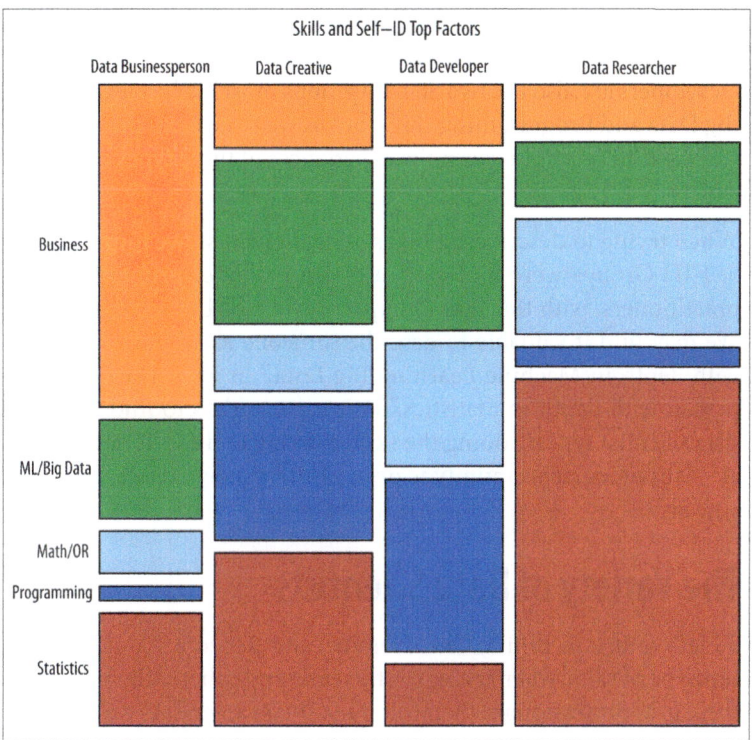

Figure 3-3. There were interesting partial correlations among each respondent's primary Skills Group (rows) and primary Self-ID Group (columns). The mosaic plot illustrates the proportions of respondents who fell into each combination of groups. For example, there were few Data Researchers whose top Skill Group was Programming.

Several reasonable observations fall out of this initial categorization. First of all, Data Businesspeople are most likely to have primarily Business-related skills. This is certainly a reassuring result. Also of note is that half of Data Businesspeople have strongest skill rankings in other areas, such as Statistics and ML/Big Data. Second, our largest group of respondents, Data Researchers, were also those most likely to have expertise in Statistics or, perhaps, Math.[1] Third, both Data Businesspeople and Data Researchers were quite unlikely to rate Programming skills as their highest skills. And fourth, Data Creatives and

---

1. Although we think our respondents cover the broad range of professionals who might be considered data scientists, we do not assert that we have an unbiased sample. Data Researchers may well not be the largest group in the population as a whole.

Data Developers demonstrated greater variability in how they ranked their skills than others (see also Figure 4-2). Data Creatives and Data Developers are also the two Self-ID groups most likely to excel in ML/Big Data and Programming skills, but as we'll see next, there are substantial differences between the experiences of these types of data scientists.

When trying to describe subtypes of data scientist, we found that the Self-ID Groups were more evocative and a better primary label for practitioners, with the Skill Groups a correlated but secondary label. We may find it valuable to describe someone as a "Data Researcher with depth in Machine Learning/Big Data," or as a "Data Businessperson with depth in Statistics." (We urge readers to find their own data scientist type by doing the skills ranking and self-ID rating tasks at survey.datacommunitydc.org (*http://survey.datacommunitydc.org/*).)

The Variety of Data Scientists

So let's return to Binita, Chao, Dmitri, and Rebecca. Could our new terms be of value when trying to efficiently and coherently speak about these four professionals, their roles, and their careers? As we've already described, Data Businesspeople, Creatives, Developers, and Researchers tend to have distinctive skills. What else can we say about them, based on their survey responses? In this section, we summarize the most interesting results.

Data Businesspeople

Data Businesspeople like Binita are those that are most focused on the organization and how data projects yield profit. They were most likely to rate themselves highly as leaders and entrepreneurs, and the most likely to have reported managing an employee (about 80% have). They were also quite likely to have done contract or consulting work, and a substantial proportion have started a business. Although they were the least likely to have an advanced degree among our respondents, with about 60% having a Master's or beyond, they were the most likely to have an MBA, at nearly 25%. But Data Businesspeople definitely have technical skills and were particularly likely, like Binita, to have undergraduate Engineering degrees. And they work with real data — about 90% report at least occasionally working on gigabyte-scale problems, which far exceeds quarterly financials in a spreadsheet. Also of note,

Data Businesspeople skewed a little older in our demographics, and nearly a quarter were female, higher than our other varieties of data scientist. But only about a quarter said they had described themselves as a "data scientist," much lower than the half of the rest of our respondents who had done so!

Data Creatives

As we'll discuss later, data scientists can often tackle the entire soup-to-nuts analytics process on their own: from extracting data, to integrating and layering it, to performing statistical or other advanced analyses, to creating compelling visualizations and interpretations, to building tools to make the analysis scalable and broadly applicable. We think of Data Creatives like Chao as the broadest of data scientists, those who excel at applying a wide range of tools and technologies to a problem, or creating innovative prototypes at hackathons — the quintessential Jack of All Trades. Our Data Creative respondents latched onto the term Artist like no other group. Similar to Data Researchers, they have substantial academic experience, with about three-quarters having taught classes and presented papers. Common undergraduate degrees were in areas like Economics and Statistics. But unlike Data Researchers, relatively few Data Creatives have a PhD. Respondents like Chao do have substantial business expertise — Data Creatives were actually slightly more likely than Data Businesspeople to have done contract work (80%) or have started a business (40%). As the group most likely to identify as a Hacker, they also had the deepest Open Source experience, with about half contributing to OSS projects and about half working on Open Data projects. We also saw that Data Creatives were somewhat younger and more likely to be male than other respondents. Curiously, they responded most positively to our final question: "Did you feel that this survey applied to you?"

Data Developer

We think of Data Developers like Dmitri as people focused on the technical problem of managing data — how to get it, store it, and learn from it. Our Data Developers tended to rate themselves fairly highly as Scientists, although not as highly as Data Researchers did. This makes sense, particularly for those closely integrated with the Machine Learning and related academic communities. But, like Dmitri, Data Developers are clearly writing code, probably production code, in their day-to-day work. About half have Computer Science or Computer Engineering degrees, and about half have contributed to Open Source projects. More Data Developers land in the Machine Learning/Big Data skills group than other types of data scientist. They were also least likely to have done consulting work, managed an employee, or contributed to an Open Data project.

Data Researchers

One of the interesting career paths that leads to a title like "data scientist" starts with academic research in the physical or social sciences, or in statistics. Many organizations have realized the value of deep academic training in the use of data to understand complex processes, even if their business domains may be quite different from classic scientific fields. People like Rebecca who end up in the Data Researchers Self-ID Group tend to be from these backgrounds. The majority of respondents whose top Skills Group was Statistics ended up in this category, for instance. Nearly 75% of Data Researchers have published in peer-reviewed journals, and over half have a PhD. (Our skewed-by-personal-connections respondents reported a surprising number of psychology and political science degrees.) On the other hand, Data Researchers were least likely to have started a business, and only half have managed an employee.

Big Data

It's worth a digression into a set of questions we asked about "big data." In our view, one of the reasons why "data science" and other buzzwords have come about recently is the advent of new technologies and techniques for inexpensively working with very large data sets. However, we also view big data as somewhat tangential to the value of data scientists to organizations. Our survey data supports this; most data scientists rarely work with terabyte or larger data. Figure 3-4 shows how often respondents worked with data of kilobyte, megabyte, gigabyte, terabyte, and petabyte scale, broken down by Skills Group (which is clearer, here, than Self-ID Group):

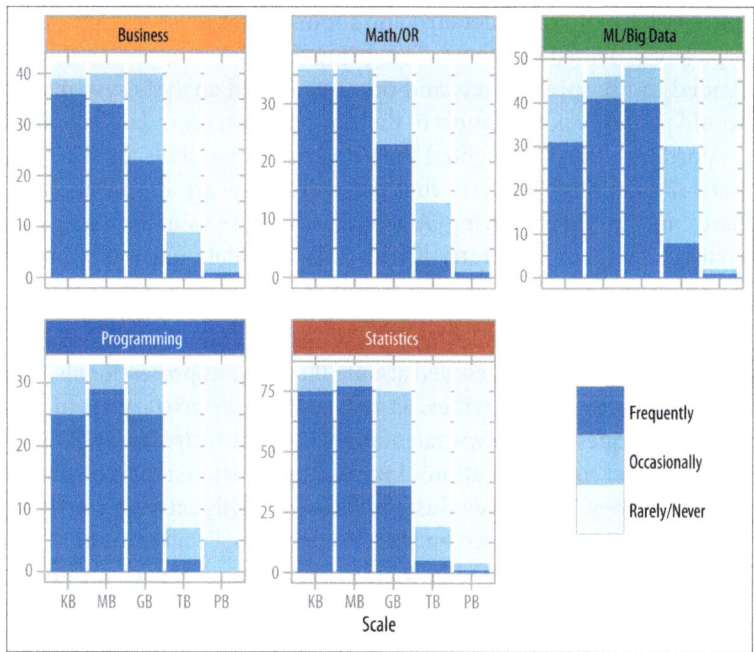

Figure 3-4. Number of respondents working with different scales of data, by primary Skills Group.

Respondents whose top Skills Group was ML/Big Data were most likely to work with larger data sets, with over half at least occasionally working on TB-scale problems, compared with about a quarter for other respondents. Even in the ML/Big Data Skills group, however, the vast majority rarely or never worked with PB-scale data. True big data work seems limited to a relatively small subset of data scientists.

Related Surveys

Among many other surveys related to data science and business analytics (e.g., Libertore and Luo, 2012 (*http://bit.ly/14oBBbh*); EMC, 2011 (*http://bit.ly/11MGj25*)), several in particular are worth noting here. Kandel et al. (2012) (*http://stanford.io/13xBOJP*) interviewed 35 "enterprise analysts" and, as part of their quantification of these interviews, identified three "archetypes": hacker, scripter, and application user. Hackers were skilled at programming and large-scale data management, and also often built sophisticated data visualizations. Scripters used statistical/mathematical programming languages like R and Matlab to do more detailed and sophisticated analyses of data sets typically provided by others. The group they called application users tended to use spreadsheets and other packaged analysis systems; we would probably not call most of these application users data scientists. Importantly, they highlighted the value of diverse skills, quoting one person as saying "analysts that can't program are disenfranchised here," and another as saying "A generalist is more valuable than a specialist... We look for pretty broad skills and data passion" (ibid, p. 2,924).

Researchers at Talent Analytics, Corp. and the International Institute for Analytics recently surveyed about 300 analytics professionals, asking about skills and activities, as well as their proprietary set of psychometric questions (www.talentanalytics.com (*http://bit.ly/ZZia4c*) and personal communication). Like us, they clustered their responses into categories. When they clustered based on daily activities, analytics professionals were focused on Data Preparation, Programming, Management, or Generalist/Other. While these categories partially line up with ours, there are substantial differences. For example, our Data Businesspeople category reported the lowest proportion of PhDs, but their Management category reported the highest proportion of PhDs. They also found psychometric patterns, such as analytics professionals overall rating highly on their curiosity dimension, but the details and the way these questions varied among their respondents remain confidential. Of note, a relatively small proportion of their respondents frequently worked with terabyte-scale data, supporting our result discussed above.

CHAPTER 4
T-Shaped Data Scientists

We feel that a defining feature of data scientists is the breadth of their skills — their ability to single-handedly do at least prototype-level versions of all the steps needed to derive new insights or build data products (Mason & Wiggins, 2010 (*http://bit.ly/10enTAO*)). We also feel that the most successful data scientists are those with substantial, deep expertise in at least one aspect of data science, be it statistics, big data, or business communication.

In many ways, this pattern matches the "T-shaped skills" idea that has been promoted since at least the early 1990s (see citations here (*http://bit.ly/109IrMw*)). The "T" represents breadth of skills, across the top, with depth in one area represented by the vertical bar. T-shaped professionals can more easily work in interdisciplinary teams than those with less breadth and can be more effective than those without depth. Data science is an inherently collaborative and creative field, where the successful professional can work with database administrators, business people, and others with overlapping skill sets to get data projects completed in innovative ways.

For data scientists, we feel this notion can help address the communications issues we've described. By clarifying your areas of depth, perhaps using our Skills terminology, others can more quickly understand where your expertise lies. We also suggest that our Skills terminology can suggest areas of career development. For instance, a data scientist with an Operations Research background and deep skills in Simulation, Optimization, Algorithms, and Math might find value in learning some of the new Bayesian/Monte Carlo Statistics methods that also fall under our Math/OR Skills Group. That same data scientist might also want to make sure they have enough broad programming, big data, and business skills to be able to intelligently collaborate with (or lead) others on a data science team.

Others have made this point as well. Stanton et al. (2012) (*http://bit.ly/ WWsVEF*), in a writeup of a recent workshop, reviewed the state of data science in a primarily academic/"eScience" context. Interestingly, they emphasized a role performing data archival and preservation, which is not currently a focus of data scientists, although perhaps it should be. Their workshop participants recommended that the breadth of T-shaped data scientists should fall into three categories: data curation, analytics and visualization, and networks and infrastructure. They also mention the intriguing idea that data scientists should have (serif) "I"-shaped skills, with domain knowledge along the bottom (see also The Data Science Venn Diagram, Conway, 2010 (*http://bit.ly/ZZkOHd*)).

Evidence for T-Shaped Data Scientists

Our survey data can be used to indicate how T-shaped data scientists already are, at least directionally. As we used rankings rather than an absolute measure of skills, our data only lets us approximate skill depth.

What would our results have to look like to support the idea that data scientists are T-shaped? In general, most respondents would have a Skill Group (e.g., Math/OR or Statistics) that they are strong in, and relatively uniform rankings in the other Skill Groups. In contrast, if the rankings (and thus groupings) were idiosyncratic, with different people having different patterns of skills, we wouldn't see that pattern.

Figure 4-1 shows that our respondents did trend toward T-shapes in their skills. Each respondent has a numerical "loading" representing the strength of their responses to the five Skill Groups. Instead of plotting the same Skill Group in the same place, we instead plot the strongest Skill Group for an individual in the center, the next strongest to the right, then to the left, and so forth. The grey bars show a subjectively created "ideal" T-shaped pattern. The grey circles illustrate a simulated null hypothesis: that our respondents were not T-shaped in their skills. (The process of sorting random ranks will naturally cause some skill groups to be stronger than others.) The green circles show the results from our respondents. They were substantially more T-shaped than you would expect from random rankings and tended to

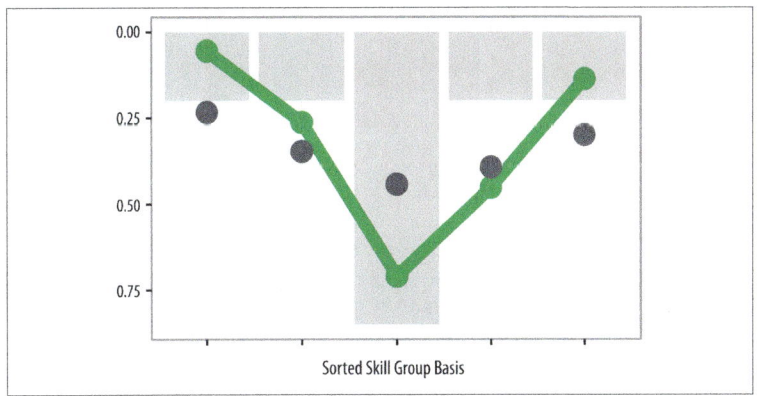

Figure 4-1. Skill Group strength for "ideal" professionals (grey bar), simulated controls (grey dots), and mean of surveyed respondents (green). Loadings are sorted from center out on a per-respondent basis.

have one strongest Skill Group, perhaps a secondary Skill Group, and weaker skills elsewhere. (See Appendix: "Non-negative Matrix Factorization" for technical details.)

We can look at the T-shaped nature of the four Self-ID Groups as well. Figure 4-2 shows how strongly, on average, people in each Self-ID Group were associated with our five Skills Groups. Data Businesspeople were quite T-shaped, with top skills in Business, and moderate skills elsewhere. Data Researchers tended to be very deep in Statistics (and related skills), but somewhat less broad. On average, they ranked all of the ML/Big Data, Business, and Programming skills fairly low. Data Developers had a pattern that might be called "Pi-shaped," with strong Programming skills and relatively strong ML/Big Data skills, along with moderate skills in the other three skill groups. And finally, Data Creatives tended to be the least T-shaped of our respondents. Interestingly, Data Creatives were, on average, neither ranked the strongest nor the weakest in any skill group.

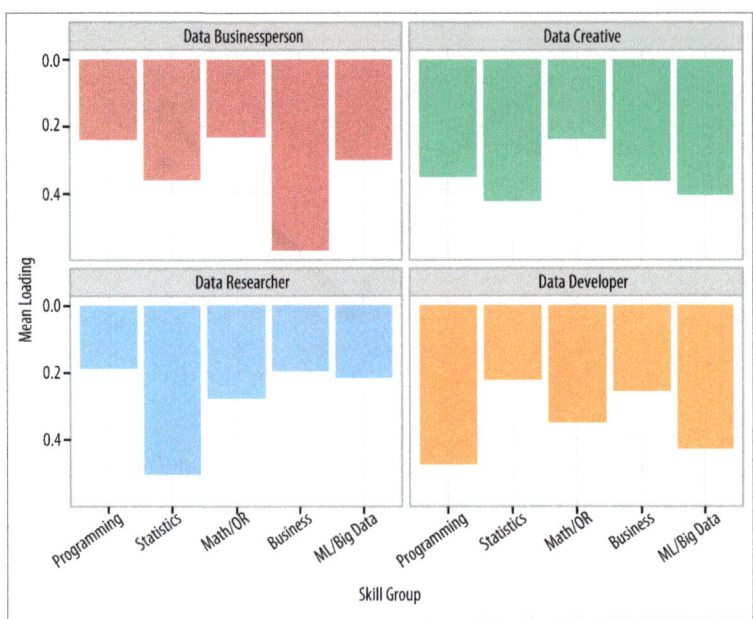

Figure 4-2. Mean Skill Group loadings for survey participants categorized into four Self-ID Groups.

CHAPTER 5
Data Scientists and Organizations

Let's turn the focus around now, and consider how our survey results might inform communication and career path problems from the point of view of organizations that need data scientists.

Where Data People Come From: Science vs. Tools Education

Tools are critical to data scientists' effectiveness. The maturity of current tools allows an individual to at least roughly perform all of the steps needed to develop insights and build data products. However, we feel that evidence points in favor of a *scientific* versus a tools-based education for data scientists. Along with technical expertise, the scientific mentoring process builds and rewards curiosity, storytelling, and cleverness (DJ Patil, 2011 (*http://oreil.ly/16hYmfa*)). Our survey results support this notion, with 70% of our respondents having at least a Master's degree, and scientific fields (social or physical sciences, but not math, computer science, statistics, or engineering) making up about 40% of reported undergraduate degrees.

Furthermore, post-graduate education in the sciences provides hands-on experience working with real data, not just to describe a phenomenon, but to evaluate a theory or argue a position. Disciplines such as physics and astronomy teach rigorous statistical thinking, while systems such as particle accelerators and space telescopes provide massive streams of data requiring careful data curation. (Data from the under-construction Square Kilometer Array telescope (*http://bit.ly/16YsBZX*) is expected to be collected at the rate of 10 PB/hour. Data from Facebook (*http://bit.ly/109LF2v*) is estimated to accumulate at the rate of less than 1 PB/day.) We feel that hard science backgrounds provide excellent training for any sort of data scientist, especially Data Developers. On the other hand, some have argued that social scientists make great data scientists too (e.g., Miller, 2012 (*http://bit.ly/16YsHkq*); Rivera, 2013 (*http://onforb.es/14vPGnq*)). Psychologists, economists, political scientists, and others work in the sort of tangled, noisy real-world data that many organizations are (unfortunately) buried in. These disciplines yield data scientists who can quickly clean and aggregate data, use advanced statistical techniques to understand causality, and think deeply about data visualization, presentation, and communication. We saw many such degrees in our Data Researcher and Data Creative respondents.

Classic Computer Science (Machine Learning) and Applied Statistics degrees can also be very effective starting points for data scientists. Machine Learning's focus on large-scale data and algorithms, combined with software development skills, apply naturally to real-world organizational data. Many Applied Statistics programs incorporate consulting, giving graduates substantial domain expertise, a critical aspect of effective data science (e.g., Conway, 2010 (*http://bit.ly/ZZkOHd*), Driscoll, 2012 (*http://bit.ly/10iLAcF*)).

It will be interesting to see the effectiveness of the new analytics, data science, and business intelligence Master's-level degrees that many colleges and universities are now starting to offer (*http://bit.ly/14oEYPn*). The history of many current data scientists are those who pivoted through a variety of fields, giving them the breadth and depth needed for the field almost accidentally. It remains to be seen whether new degrees will offer the scope and practicality to provide the software engineering, statistical thinking, and domain skills needed to be immediately effective, or if additional experience will be necessary.

From Theory to Practice: Internships and Mentoring

As with many other fields, moving from academia to practice in data science can be tricky. Patil (2011) (*http://oreil.ly/16hYmfa*) suggests "[taking] incredibly bright and creative people right out of college and [putting] them through a very robust internship program." For large organizations with the budget and senior talent to lead that sort of program, this could work very well, but it seems unlikely to us to be scalable down.

An interesting alternative model, highlighted at DataGotham 2012 (*http://bit.ly/WWuS3S*), is the hiring consultant who helps to recruit, train, and then integrate and mentor a fresh-out-of-school data scientist in a smaller organization. DonorsChoose.org (*http://www.donorschoose.org/*), realizing they needed a data scientist to get the best value from data collected as part of their charitable mission, worked with an expert data scientist over a roughly five-month period. Before the hire, the expert helped the nonprofit understand the role of a data scientist, and afterward helped train and mentor the new employee, and set a path forward for successful initial projects. We feel that the broad talents of data scientists will be useful for small organizations, but that innovative approaches such as this will be necessary to assure effectiveness.

Teams and Org Charts

We have heard a number of anecdotes about data scientists whose effectiveness was hampered due to inadequate integration with the rest of the organization. There are several aspects to this. First, as suggested by our data showing the diversity of data scientists, and the typical T-shaped distribution of skills, data scientists should work in teams with overlapping skills to be most effective (Davenport et al., 2010 (*http://amzn.to/Zxm9VL*); Patil, 2011 (*http://oreil.ly/16hYmfa*)). As we described in the introduction, there is an occasional tendency for organizations that don't understand this to want to hire a "god" who can do it all.

Another aspect of integration is the need for organizations to set up their data science teams so that they can work effectively. Patil (2011) (*http://oreil.ly/16hYmfa*) again: "A new hire won't do something amazing, now or in the future, if the organization he or she works for doesn't hold up its end of the bargain. The organization must provide a platform and opportunities for the individual to be successful." Data science teams need direct access to both raw data and decision-makers, and based on our analysis, they need a diversity of skills to make best use of that access. They also need to be supported by a management with a process for adopting and using their results. Projects whose potential outcomes cannot be turned into organizational change will probably never pay for themselves. When the output of a data science team is expected to be software with a full life-cycle, it is critical that the team include from the beginning adequate resources to test, deploy, and maintain the system. Although some of our respondents had the Programming Skills to attempt some of those tasks, it is unrealistic to expect that most Data Businesspeople or Data Researchers could do so effectively on their own. In larger organizations, the funding and managerial relationship between analytics teams and the rest of the business, including data infrastructure and IT staff, can be critically important to realizing the benefits of data science (Davenport et al., 2010 (*http://amzn.to/Zxm9VL*)).

Career Paths

There are several concerns that organizations may have when constructing not just static roles for data scientists, but career paths with opportunities for advancement. As with many classes of employees, data scientists with years of experience and domain expertise can be both extremely valuable and extremely hard to replace. The engineering professions have long considered the pros and cons of promotion into management roles, and identified viable alternatives for senior people who do not want to manage. Of our respondents, 62% have managed others; it would be interesting to know how many data scientists aspire to manage teams, versus find management an annoyance.

A potentially interesting approach to keeping data scientists engaged in large organizations is to set up a job rotation program (Davenport et al., 2010 (*http://amzn.to/Zxm9VL*)). After an initial orientation period, data scientists could be systematically rotated among internal teams. A product group may need a personalization model; a marketing group may need help with controlled experiments; a finance group may need help with forecasting; an operations group may need help with process optimization. By being embedded directly in the group, a data scientist can learn critical business values and skills, focus on problems that a group most needs help with, and provide solutions with minimal distraction. But, by being rotated periodically, a data scientist can gain a valuable breadth of skills and points of view, while continuing to develop their deepest Skills Group.

CHAPTER 6
Final Thoughts

After considering themselves and their careers in the framework we have suggested here, Binita, Chao, Dmitri, and Rebecca all made some changes. Binita learned some clearer ways of talking about the diversity of people on her team and will help HR to more clearly define roles, at least until she leaves to strike out on her own. Chao sees the value in specializing more and will be signing up for some massive open online courses (MOOCs) to deepen his Statistics skills. He hopes to complement his existing visualization skillset with some work in time-series modeling. Dmitri, conversely, sees some benefit in diversifying a bit and will start to read more about data visualization technology and about how to sell data projects to managers. Rebecca has identified some process and organizational changes in her company that would help her be more effective and will start chatting with managers about how those might happen.

Others benefited from this framework too. That CEO who was looking for a "god" got his expectations in line with reality and is now looking to build a small, diverse data science team. And the firm that confused Binita's Data Businessperson skills with those of a Data Developer has a newfound appreciation for the variety of people in this field and the variety of talents that they bring to the table.

We hope that our work can be valuable to the community broadly, but we realize that this article is just one step forward. Our suggested names for the variety of data scientist are just suggestions. Additional survey research could help clarify the natural categories more clearly, and we look forward to data illustrating how the field is changing over time, as new educational and career paths emerge.

APPENDIX A
Survey Details

Design and Invitation

The survey was created on KwikSurveys.com (note: hacked, closed, and reopened under new management since we used it). The first page described the survey, stated our privacy policy, and thanked participants. The second page posed the skills-sorting task. The third page asked about education and experiences. The fourth page asked about professional web presence. The fifth page asked about self-identification and had some basic demographic questions. The final page thanked the participant and provided a link to send to others.

After testing, we posted links on social and professional networking sites, emailed friends and colleagues, and so forth. A sample personal invitation was:

> As someone in the broad Analytics / Data Science / Big Data / Applied Stats / Machine Learning space, would you be willing to take a brief survey? Three of us in the DC Data Science community wondered about the ways that skills and experiences of practitioners in these fields vary, and are collecting some data to help us learn more. By participating, you would help us define these new fields better, and we hope the results will help people such as yourself talk about how your skills and your work fit in with everyone else's. Should take 10 minutes or less!

Skills List

Here are the list of skills we provided (in random order) and asked respondents to sort:

- Algorithms (ex: computational complexity, CS theory)
- Back-End Programming (ex: JAVA/Rails/Objective C)
- Bayesian/Monte-Carlo Statistics (ex: MCMC, BUGS)
- Big and Distributed Data (ex: Hadoop, Map/Reduce)
- Business (ex: management, business development, budgeting)
- Classical Statistics (ex: general linear model, ANOVA)
- Data Manipulation (ex: regexes, R, SAS, web scraping)
- Front-End Programming (ex: JavaScript, HTML, CSS)
- Graphical Models (ex: social networks, Bayes networks)
- Machine Learning (ex: decision trees, neural nets, SVM, clustering)
- Math (ex: linear algebra, real analysis, calculus)
- Optimization (ex: linear, integer, convex, global)
- Product Development (ex: design, project management)
- Science (ex: experimental design, technical writing/publishing)
- Simulation (ex: discrete, agent-based, continuous)
- Spatial Statistics (ex: geographic covariates, GIS)
- Structured Data (ex: SQL, JSON, XML)
- Surveys and Marketing (ex: multinomial modeling)
- Systems Administration (ex: *nix, DBA, cloud tech.)
- Temporal Statistics (ex: forecasting, time-series analysis)
- Unstructured Data (ex: noSQL, text mining)
- Visualization (ex: statistical graphics, mapping, web-based dataviz)

Non-negative Matrix Factorization

We used Non-negative Matrix Factorization (*http://bit.ly/11NqiVW*) to perform our Skills and Self-ID clusterings. NMF attempts to find a matrix factorization where all elements of the basis vectors are constrained to be non-negative. This is natural in data sets such as our skills rankings, which range from 0 (lowest or missing) to 21 (highest).

The R NMF package that we used is not currently available via CRAN, but can be downloaded (*http://bit.ly/YE8PlS*) from the archives.

We used the standard Brunet et al. (2004) method, which attempts to minimize KL-divergence. Note that NMF attempts to globally optimize a non-smooth function from a random initial state, and so we used 200 random runs to find a relatively reliable factorization. (See main text for several skills/self-ID terms that sometimes fell into other groups when different random seeds were chosen. These small differences did not appreciably affect our overall results.) The ranks of 5 and 4 (for Skills and Self-ID, respectively) were chosen to maximize the informativeness and interpretability (evaluated subjectively) of the resulting basis vectors. Lower ranks yielded vague factors, while higher ranks yielded less informative results compared to the raw ranks/ratings.

The results of NMF are two matrices: a *coefficients* matrix that describes how the observed dimensions can be approximately reconstructed with a smaller number of latent factors, and a *basis* matrix that describes how individual respondents' rankings/ratings can be approximately summarized using the latent factors. We categorize individual respondents by normalizing the basis matrix and selecting the largest latent factor loading. The normalized coefficients matrix is used to assign skills/self-ID terms to Skill Groups/Self-ID Groups.

For T-shaped skills analysis, we use the normalized basis vectors for each respondent. Figure 4-1 was constructed by multiplying 1,000 simulated random rankings of skills by the computed coefficients matrix to get skill group loadings for each simulated respondent. For both that matrix and the observed basis matrix we then sorted the normalized loadings from high to low, then plotted the means in the following order (left-to-right): 5, 3, 1, 2, 4.

Acknowledgements

Thank you to those who gave us valuable feedback on drafts of this article and the survey, to those who gave us opportunities to share the results, as well as to our hundreds of survey participants around the world. Particular thanks to: MB, DC, AD, AF, NK, JDL, HM, NN, DJP, NT, KV, JW, JMW, and EZ.

—*Harlan Harris, Sean Murphy, and Marck Vaisman*

About the Authors

Harlan D. Harris is a data scientist with experience in predictive modeling, software design, statistics, social science, operations, marketing, and simulation. He is the co-founder and co-organizer of the Data Science DC Meetup, and the co-founder and President of Data Community DC, Inc. He has a PhD in Computer Science from the University of Illinois at Urbana-Champaign and worked as a researcher in several Psychology departments before turning to industry.

Sean Patrick Murphy, with degrees in mathematics, electrical engineering, and biomedical engineering and an MBA from Oxford University, has served as a senior scientist at the Johns Hopkins Applied Physics Laboratory for the past 10 years. Previously, he served as the Chief Data Scientist at WiserTogether, a series A funded health care analytics firm, and the Director of Research at Manhattan Prep, a boutique graduate educational company. He was also the co-founder and CEO of a big data-focused startup: CloudSpree.

Marck Vaisman is a data scientist, consultant, entrepreneur, master munger, and hacker. Marck is the Principal Data Scientist at DataXtract, LLC helping clients from start-ups to Fortune 500 firms with all kinds of data science projects. His professional experience spans the management consulting, telecommunications, Internet, and technology industries. He is the co-founder of Data Community DC, Inc. and co-organizer of the Data Science DC and R Users DC Meetup groups. He has an MBA from Vanderbilt University and a B.S. in Mechanical Engineering from Boston University. Marck is also a contributing author of *The Bad Data Handbook*.

Have it your way.

O'Reilly eBooks

- Lifetime access to the book when you buy through oreilly.com
- Provided in up to four DRM-free file formats, for use on the devices of your choice: PDF, .epub, Kindle-compatible .mobi, and Android .apk
- Fully searchable, with copy-and-paste and print functionality
- Alerts when files are updated with corrections and additions

oreilly.com/ebooks/

Safari Books Online

- Access the contents and quickly search over 7000 books on technology, business, and certification guides
- Learn from expert video tutorials, and explore thousands of hours of video on technology and design topics
- Download whole books or chapters in PDF format, at no extra cost, to print or read on the go
- Get early access to books as they're being written
- Interact directly with authors of upcoming books
- Save up to 35% on O'Reilly print books

See the complete Safari Library at safari.oreilly.com

O'REILLY®

Spreading the knowledge of innovators.   oreilly.com

©2011 O'Reilly Media, Inc. O'Reilly logo is a registered trademark of O'Reilly Media, Inc. 00000

Get even more for your money.

Join the O'Reilly Community, and register the O'Reilly books you own. It's free, and you'll get:

- $4.99 ebook upgrade offer
- 40% upgrade offer on O'Reilly print books
- Membership discounts on books and events
- Free lifetime updates to ebooks and videos
- Multiple ebook formats, DRM FREE
- Participation in the O'Reilly community
- Newsletters
- Account management
- 100% Satisfaction Guarantee

Signing up is easy:

1. Go to: oreilly.com/go/register
2. Create an O'Reilly login.
3. Provide your address.
4. Register your books.

Note: English-language books only

To order books online:
oreilly.com/store

For questions about products or an order:
orders@oreilly.com

To sign up to get topic-specific email announcements and/or news about upcoming books, conferences, special offers, and new technologies:
elists@oreilly.com

For technical questions about book content:
booktech@oreilly.com

To submit new book proposals to our editors:
proposals@oreilly.com

O'Reilly books are available in multiple DRM-free ebook formats. For more information:
oreilly.com/ebooks

Spreading the knowledge of innovators   oreilly.com

©2010 O'Reilly Media, Inc. O'Reilly logo is a registered trademark of O'Reilly Media, Inc. 00000

CPSIA information can be obtained at www.ICGtesting.com
Printed in the USA
BVOW11s1408040215

386250BV00001BA/3/P